It Was Best Left Unsaid

Clarice Rider

Published by Clarice Rider, 2024.

IT WAS BEST LEFT UNSAID

First edition. February 5, 2024.

Copyright © 2024 Clarice Rider.

ISBN: 979-8224073603

Written by Clarice Rider.

Table of Contents

To my many muses-- beautiful and ugly. I've created pretty words out of you all.

The Fatal Wound Between My Legs

The bed is warm, as it is basked in morning light.
Warmed by bodies and the sun,
I run my hand against your pillow,
Expecting to trail my fingers against your face.
I find not flesh, but fabric cooled by dawn.
You are no longer beside me.
When you begged to spend a night with me,
I foolishly assumed it would run into morning.
But to you 'spend a night' means sleep.
No. Not sleep. That's not what you were after.
I extended my body to you.
In a spiritual act of physical intimacy.
And now you are gone. Having claimed what it was you were after.
In the overbearing light of morning, I see blood staining my blanket.
My blood. That you had drawn from me.
In the moment, it had been so gentle.
Now I am injured as if from war.
My body, just as maimed as that, of a fallen soldier.
The bed is warm, in pools of drying blood.

Anorexic Enticement

I lost religion when I was fourteen.
   Too young to know my own body,
   I starved Jesus right out of me.
   I purged out my soul as I binged in sins.
   And then the tactics came to keep Him away.
   The boys, who became idols.
   When I got on my knees for them,
   It was never in holy reverence.
   Then sour wines drenched my tongue,
   Slurred my speech until I could no longer
   Preach in ways that made me believe.
   And bitter weed stained my lips,
   Like poison, it felt like a warning to the predators—
   Nothing about me is enticing.

Broken Stem

He says my spine is akin to a rose,
>A former lover's favorite flower.
>The way that I was born deformed,
>Romantic in its own right.
>Haunting me throughout my life.
>My back arching, the pain shooting to my heart.
>His strong fingers picked at the thorns.
>He says it makes me lovely,
>But I doubt that's the first time he's used those words.
>The idea that he could speak in poems,
>To the women whom he'd loved before,
>Appalls me. Can love be true,
>When it is repeated?
>And when my broken body draws memories of other women,
>Is the taste of my flower lips truly sweet?
>Or is it just fermented, the bitter remnant of her tongue?

Fallout of Temptation

Soft facade of an angel,
    Almost feminine in your care.
    Unprepared, but enticing,
    We would learn the world together.
    And then you had my kiss,
    Like your first earthly prize,
    And heaven seemed less enticing,
    With my body on your mind.
    Suddenly you fell away from the place
    Where you'd been sent,
    And satan stood up on his throne,
    And preyed on your descent.
    I watched as you slipped away,
    From the innocent life you'd known,
    And took up a new cause,
    To conquer the heavenly crown.
    Temptation came easy,
    Turning you away,
    From boy of little knowledge
    To a man with passionate rage.

Father, father

I'm scared that I will love a man who resembles my father.
Claiming a strength in his inability to control his anger.
Self-righteous because he is pious. Using God to justify his wrongs.
The sermons I've heard about his sins,
And once he leaves the pulpit I see no shame.
His repentance a temporary act,
His humility disappearing before his children.
We are small and he is a domineering force,
Of course, we obey him. Head of the household,
As God commanded.
His place of honor, justified by misinterpretation.
The amount of times as a little girl, I cried before him,
Even as an adult, tears run down my face if I hear him raise his voice
from another room.
Growing up, I prayed for peace,
Now I ask for him to calm his demeanor.
We all have pet sins, I do not claim to be faultless.
But I try not to inflict suffering to others with mine.

How I Felt in March

Unrequited passion, a fault that I have damned
    And yet I'd sacrifice my soul, for just touch of his dear hand.
    As his body draws now nearer, my breath begins to still.
    Forgetting all my morals, my empathy he'll kill.
    Intoxicated by his presence, I'm no longer me at all.
    I am the woman— against whom my hatred previously'd burned.
    I would have called her selfish, now she's tragic, fallen hero.
    For you could not accuse me, my love for him's not evil.
    And since I cannot have him, I'll lie my murder on his hands,
    Lying on my deathbed, my conqueror, he stands.
    Since he failed to love me, I've lost all I once had.
    My straying, hopeless heart, my soul in hell be damned.

I Will Disappoint My Daughter

I have nothing, I'm sedated.
Sober and somber from grief.
Life's changing, can't accept it,
Nature's form of infidelity.
Ironic though it is, withdrawn I will remain.
Why give away my heart, when only grief I'll gain?
Knowledgeable are you, promising to love me for my life,
But lifespan of a woman lasts only until she is "wife"
Then suddenly all leave her, she's caught in her own storm.
Forcing years of hardships, onto the children she has borne.
And nothing tells of trials, more than marriages that never cease.
For a woman's love will last, even through her grief.
She is scared to become her mother, watching as she sacrificed.
And now she does the same, trying to protect her babes new life.
And hatred slowly grows, as men all seem to cease.
Her husband never loved her, just craved a family.
Now she is sentenced, to live as she always feared,
Her new born daughter knowing, that she's not a cycle breaker.

Liquid Woman

Fluidity of a woman,
    Smooth like the water in the basin that I pour.
    Her body flows as if persuaded
    By wind, or the dancing ember of a dying fire.
    Light touch,
    Gentle on my skin, a kiss that warms my body.
    And still the river flows,
    From the mouth of her porcelain jar.
    Washing me anew,
    Baptizing me outside of my religion.
    This is pure.
    This is clean— remedy to my past love.
    Making my heart empty,
    Absorbing only her.

Love in Deeper Words

She lays stiffly beneath you,
    Your passion not inspiring her.
    And the words you speak as poems,
    Building up your future. The wall that divides you.
    Your eloquence, the final straw that damns her love.
    How dare her lover speak in riddles?
    But I am eager to unravel your tongue,
    To decipher the mystery of your heart.
    To kiss you until the words pour out,
    To offer my being as your personal muse.
    Are we too alike in that way? Creating art from existence?
    Is it romantic to craft a life off of pleasure and pain?
    To crave extremes, the furthest peaks of emotion.
    And what if we run out of language?
    When every combination of letters has been spoken,
    Will we remain true? Or will passion wane?
    I'll just kiss you harder, give you more of me.
    We will write again, speak, praise, love in poetry.

Lust and Vanity

I like the feeling of eyes on me.
Hungry, jealous, full of lust.
It's because of how I was raised—
woefully repressed by my religion.
Shamed for the simple act of looking in a mirror.
Apparently, as a child, my body had a forbidden sense of allure
I grew to believe that I had power,
Control over even the most pious of men.
It had never occurred to me, that these men were greedy
Tempted by their eyes, working deftly through their hands.
And when he first grabbed me, I realized that being a woman
wasn't a power after all.
And when my father told me to not be vain,
In a twisted way, he was trying to protect me from his own kind.

Marred

You marked me as your lover,
    Leaving wounds upon my flesh.
    And you will not heal the bruises,
    Rather revel in the way they look upon my breast.
    It's not the fact you love me, that is openly displayed,
    But the fact that someone uses me, is printed on my face.
    It is disgustingly ill-romantic,
    To watch your hungry eyes take pride.
    You mark me not as yours. But as a slut— a stolen prize.
    Walking into church,
    I felt eyes keenly take me in,
    And the piercing blue of the pastor's son,
    Watched as I bore my sin.
    I kneeled in deep confession, as I downed communion wine,
    My Savior's sticky blood, poured down my throat,
    As if *this* was why he died.
    And I prayed for absolution, for my multitude of sins.
    Then walking out into the morning light made me feel almost forgiven.

Mary Magdalene

My hair is saturated in oil,
Much too rich for me to afford.
I place my hand over my empty, aching stomach
As I bend down to anoint the feet of my Lord.
I revere this man, who took pity on me.
Who was willing to be seen in my company,
Who never dared to make a move to touch me.
Even when we were alone, propriety always ruled.
I think that is why I love him so dearly.
Because he treats me as every other woman is treated.
Below him? Yes. But a human nonetheless.
My thick curls are absorbing dust along with excess oil when He suddenly makes the claim, "I am the son of God."
This is obviously not the first time he has told me this.
I revere him in an almost holy light, so why not allow this blasphemy to flow from his lips?
"This woman," he pulls to me to my feet beside him,
I appear as if his equal. "Is the example of how you all should live."
Has this great man forgotten about my multitude of sins?
My hunger and empty pockets draw me back to my place.
Humbled, I seat myself at the Lambs feet,
Watching as he, and twelve other men feast.

Okay, Maybe I Sent Some of Them

I wrote you letters,
> Despite the fact I knew you would never read them.
> I wasted an abundance of my words,
> On a man too dense to appreciate deeper meaning.
> And even though within my spiraling print,
> I promised you my heart,
> My handwriting does little to conceal,
> The contents of my soul.
> Printed in the papers, the world has seen my hand,
> And now the odds that I could secure another man?
> On you I wasted wisdom, dignity, and bliss.
> For you, I wrote letters,
> But they were never sent.

Park Times and Raspberry Tea

We are not bound by blood,
    No physical entity forcing us to love,
    And yet we do.
    I feel as if you are a continuation of myself.
    Like we are two rivers, joined at one mouth,
    One bank holds us, where we meet.
    And nightly we reminisce,
    On a former life, before the rocks between us
    Corroded away. Our waters lap against
    A shared shore. Waves crashing in laughter.
    And love is freely, constantly given.
    Together, we watch other waters,
    Waters large, like oceans,
    And we protest their strength.
    We could also drown a hundred sailors with our might,
    But we'd rather sit with their sails, beautiful against a pink horizon.
    Morning has come, and dawn paints our waters,
    Pretty like the sky, two entities,
    Stained together as one.

It Was Best Left Unsaid

"Oh my love" you cry, eyes filled with horror as you stare down at my body.

"My love!" Again. Crocodile tears falling in a flood around me.

If the dead could drown, you would kill me again.

The coroner pushes you aside, he is gentle and kind in his mannerisms.

He buys the act that you put on.

That's funny. I think. Because you are a horrible actor.

You tried to make it on the stage, but the audience could see right through you.

"My love," you will not stop. Nothing can silence you as my body is carried away.

At my funeral, I am faintly aware of my body being placed into the grave.

For a final time, I hear your damned voice "I need you."

A weight is pressed down on me. It is not dirt, but your decaying body.

You are also dead?

Perhaps you did love me after all. I'm sorry for believing otherwise.

Premature Discovery

I didn't know what sex was until after I was assaulted.
    Not because I was so young,
    But because my mother left me tragically ignorant.
    Wanting to preserve my piety,
    She sheltered me from words of sin.
    I knew not how to make love,
    But I knew to abhor the touch of man.
    So when he grasped for my breasts,
    I believed that I had fallen to temptation.
    And when I fought against his strength,
    I had sealed my condemnation.
    "Get off me," and "No!" echoed through the room.
    And he whispered in my ear, all the dirty things he desired to do.
    A girl, at fifteen, is on the brink of being a woman,
    And somehow in that moment,
    I could form an image of my body,
    Contorted against his. Unnatural and unwilling–
    Is that how it always is?
    No wonder my mom thought to hide the reality from me.
    The violence of man, and corruption of his desires.
    He wanted my body cold, buried completely in snow.
    Longed for me to be more helpless than I already felt.
    These things that he told me built in me a fear,
    And every time he touched me, I felt my purity disappear.
    Though he never forced me to go "all the way,"
    It seemed as though he'd already seen me completely on display.
    My body, not so sacred, defiled by his hands,
    I scratched my skin open until it wept and bled.
    I've healed now, scars covering the sensation of his fingers,
    Marred skin, a reminder of a poor girl's ignorance.

IT WAS BEST LEFT UNSAID

Some nights I wake up fearing that he will come to claim my virginity, still.

Years and years later, I truly fear he will.

Self Love

I had fallen in love with my art,
    Believing the muse to be my passion.
    Reading back now, poems that are addressed to you,
    They are an ode to myself. The creator.
    I now see why editors called me tragic,
    Why they urged me to leave the man
    Who inspired my painful words.
    Why? I had thought, Why give up my greatness
    You were never my strength.
    A temporary fixation.
    I confused inspiration with romance,
    Tragedy with lust.
    The way I loved my craft, manifested in a man.

Self Sacrifice?

Your hands are greedy—
    But not as desperate as my heart.
    My face flushes in seldom-felt humiliation
    As your fingers find the concealed curve of my waist.
    I once regarded my body as sacred- now it's so easily exposed.
    You have a claim to it, which I allowed through compromise
    I give you my physical being in the moment,
    Someday, you'll repay me with your love.
    We aren't built for forever, but I dream of it anyway.
    Once you leave me, drained of once holy virtue,
    I'll repent of it. Until then, you may have me.
    Setting my morals aside to appease you,
    A form of manipulation— I give you everything all I want in return
is your love.

Feeding My Hunger

I ate the scraps from her hand when she gave me you,
    Like I was starving– not like– I was starving.
    She got bored and handed you away.
    My hungry body quickly found refuge in you.
    I had believed myself her superior.
    Sure you loved her first, she had bigger breasts, blonder hair, bluer
eyes, a perfect face–
    But my waist was smaller.
    The inches of my stomach were much less significant than hers.
    So I believed that I had won.
    Because a portion of my body was thinner,
    That made me more deserving of your love.
    I licked the crumbs of you from her manicured fingers,
    My own nails broken and brittle from malnutrition.
    A previous obsession with numbers– calories, weight,
    Turned to my fixation on you.
    A man who began to bolster my sense of self.
    Without you, I was nothing but a frail body,
    Love and starvation always shared a space in my head.

The Collar I Grab When I Kiss

Every time we kiss I fear that it will be the last.
    So my lips find yours with renewed fervor,
    Hoping that the taste of my love will stay branded past the time of
our encounter.
    Every time I walk away, I promise myself I will end things.
    Your memory stains my skin, and when you are gone,
    I long for your corrosive touch once again.
    The drugs in your system have me hooked,
    I'm addicted to our painful love.
    The love that I inspire, I will let it carry on.
    Maybe I will end things tomorrow, after a final, gentle kiss goodbye.

The Wide Range of A Man's Love

A humbling experience for a woman
Is when she throws herself to the ground,
Begging for her lover to extend his heart.
In groveling submission he obliges,
Only to suffocate her in a kiss.
"This is love," he explains.
He acts as if it is a gift.
With tears, she answers,
"Love is when you listen.
Love is when you hold me,
Love is when I am a woman."
"I am a man." He replies,
An angry smile on his face. He calls it pride.
She sees the expression as his wrath.
With tears in her eyes, she looks up at him.
"Yes. This is love." And she kisses him.
His hold constricts her heart.
She knows no other than the love of a man.

Too Old for Kissing

Widowed, before I have become a wife.
    I stare at you in torment, as you confess,
    That you have never loved me.
    The desire to kiss a woman,
    To be embraced in her warmth,
    But not to have a future.
    You're not ready to grow up,
    You just want to be a little boy.
    How dare I betray you by acting mature.
    I swear I can change,
    Cater to your needs.
    You shake your head, disgusted by my tears.
    The accusation that I am an adult burns.
    But I know it is true, I'm an eldest daughter.
    I've been acting as a mother since I was three.
    Do not blame me for this fault, blame my father.
    Who saw me as a woman since I was a little girl.
    Made me cook dinners, fold laundry, and watch babies,
    Even when I was too young to care for myself.
    Sure I am a woman now, but I was when I was younger too.
    Nothing has changed.
    Kiss me without your commitment,
    So that I can feel like a child for the first time.

[Guilty Conscience]

Guilty conscience,
    Guilty soul,
    A pentalientant heart
    The grief of death
    And dark decay
    Rots deep within my bones
    Pretty face,
    Pretty soul,
    My lover once so fair
    My hands now covered
    In her blood
    Once innocent and rare
    Dirt and soot
    Are intertwined
    In my own back plot
    Her ashes poured
    Into my garden
    Her life becomes a single rose

[He is like a Little Cabin]

He is like a little cabin
    In the middle of the woods.
    Abandoned- say, forgotten
    I'll visit it in summer, once
    It'll do us both some good
    His empty dusty rooms, a very empty home
    But for a week of summer I'll pretend
    That this is life- he is my home.
    Then rolls around August,
    With bitter biting winds,
    His shelter is not stable for me to winter in
    Once again he'll go unnoticed,
    Until the icy snow melts,
    Then our cycle, we'll repeat it.
    I cannot stay away- his love is like my house

[I Killed Her Love, Swift Motion]

I killed her love, swift motion,
    Was an easy sort of thing.
    Grasping her emotions,
    Draining her disdains.
    She fell for my delusions,
    What a stupid girl
    I have her in my hands now,
    I'll manipulate her soul.
    Crushing each red organ,
    With bitter fingers, strong,
    Her heart is my new plaything,
    Leading her affections on.
    So shall she never love me?
    I shouldn't seem to care,
    I have her heart, unknowing,
    I'll be the victim here.

[In Our Secret Garden]

In our secret garden
    We said our last goodbyes
    Our broken solitude
    Split up by desperate cries
    I begged for you to stay
    For one more perfect night
    So you picked for me a flower,
    And swore we'd be 'alright'
    My sacred flower wilted,
    Void of your holy touch
    As the flower cried out for water,
    I was hopeless for your love

Starving God

Beauty is what you make it,
    And to me it was my master.
    It corrupted all I once had,
    A lustful sense of control
    I purged myself of pleasures,
    Of sustenance— I watched myself fade
    But the ugly beast of beauty praised my ambition
    As physically I became less,
    Spiritually, I was more.
    I believed myself to be enlightened.
    Being higher, I had found control.

Suicidal Worship

If I were a pagan,
    You would be my moon.
    The goddess whom I worship,
    Would fall second place to you.
    I would live in a castle,
    Grand but weathered and old,
    My bare feet falling against broken cobblestone.
    My curtains torn from years of being thrown against the sun,
    Now opening my window to reveal the beams of dusk.
    Because if I were a pagan— I would collect your healing rays.
    My body is the object, and you the artist that it praises.
    And in the theme of ritual you would watch as my frame,
    Falls from the highest tower, and into the inky lake.

Unread Love Letters

Was it ill romantic to write to you,
When you could barely read?
Or did I create a beauty,
Within ironic tragedy?
I offered to recite aloud,
Every heartfelt word,
But your ego and your pride,
Forced you to decline my love.
Was it not the sweetest thing,
A woman had ever done,
To deny her modern world,
And instead regress to your shadow.
I quit my dreams, abstained from passions,
All so that you could have me at your ransom.
Your request was all I wished,
I'd serve you at your feet,
Call out to me, your woman,
And groveling, there I'd be.
In my own handwriting, ink smudged
From pull of my hand, I gave you
A letter. With the hope that you could understand.

Wedding Gifts

I wanted to burn everything you gave me,
 Former feelings consumed by flame,
 But for all the time I had loved you
 There was no tangible form of proof.
 Yes, there were letters that I had composed.
 Stored them in a shoebox under my bed,
 A post it note on the lid reading "for my future husband."
 Declarations of love, but never addressed to you.
 Intentionally, I had never written your name,
 In fear that you would cease to love me.
 It would be wrong, to give those letters
 To another man, when my heart was with you when they were written,
 But something about the idea of destroying my own creative work feels wrong.
 My love for you is evidence that I can feel,
 That I am not incapable of simple emotions.
 The only physical remnant of our relationship
 Is a box of letters, addressed to any man who marries me.
 I'll burn them to celebrate my wedding.

False Woman

Your touch is that of a woman's,
Carefully curated and well practiced after your past experiences.
You've learned to replicate the soft caress,
An attempt at feminine fluidity, trying to steal into my heart.
Your fingers against my back in the moonlight,
The way they trailed down my skin,
Proving that you can never love me like a real man.
A false front you've projected, so I would entrust you with my body.
To a true man, however, he would effortlessly claim my soul.
You may love me like a woman, but your greed is that of a boy.

[Decaying Flowers Rancid]

Decaying flowers rancid,
　　Disgrace to living things
　　Defile nature's beauty,
　　With their infidelity.
　　Like scarlet drops of sinful
　　Temptation- growing scorn
　　The once life captivated flowers
　　Posses beauty little more,
　　And yet she seems to grasp it,
　　A tender kind of ache,
　　Seeing it as lovely,
　　The flowers die, a bodily change

Philanthropy

His wife was much too pretty
    For me to understand
    How even in her heels,
    In his shadows where she'd stand
    He wasn't even strong-
    Just had a lot of power,
    The fact that she had children
    Whom he didn't father
    He was her only chance
    At good society
    And a man like him was caring
    For her social needs.
    He took her in, and trained her
    Now she just obeys
    A pretty smile always plastered
    On her hurting face

[I am so Envious of the Sun]

I am so envious of the sun
      That gets to dip down
      And kiss along your skin
      The radiant shine around you,
      That you are basking in
      The loveliness of nature
      Cannot compare to you,
      You have won the earth's favor,
      So you alone possess my heart,
      You oh man, who's greater than the stars

[In the Middle of the Ocean]

In the middle of the ocean
    With the hungry waves and wind
    The boat is moving forward,
    While the stern is slowly sinking
    In our final desperate breaths,
    We kiss before our watery deaths
    As my cold and bony fingers cling to you,
    You know we'll share the same deep tomb
    They'll find us in the lake
    Many years from now
    Our bodies still together,
    Not far out from the bow
    They'll separate our timeless grasp
    Bury us each beneath the grass,
    Eternally in a soundless rest

[My Fiance, She is Riding]

My fiance, she is riding,
    In her wedding gown
    We will be wed by morning,
    It's the talk of all the town
    Her body paled and somber,
    Death painted her in grief,
    The woman's corpse, still lovely,
    I'm wedding the deceased.
    Tomorrow in her coffin,
    We'll be together in the ground.
    Flowers fit for funerals,
    The irony resounds

[To be a Woman is to Sacrifice]

To be a woman is to sacrifice.
    I give up myself to become you,
    And that is a woman's love.
    For the rest of my life I am you,
    Until I die, I transform– for love.
    For my husband, for my children
    I am them, no longer myself.
    To be a woman is to change,
    Because imitation is the highest form of flattery

A Romantic Sort of Death

My body isn't a temple it's a dirty funeral pyre
    And all the voices in my head scream to "start it all on fire"
    Skip a meal or two, watch the hungry flames climb higher
    Sleepless nights and stupid fights all on a funeral pyre
    I've always fancied death in an innocent desperate way
    Imagining my body draped elegantly beneath a flame
    Jagged broken bones under torn up dirty clothes, but who am I to
blame
    A body once so perfect completely burnt away, all on a funeral pyre
    I crave death with such a passion it makes me go insane
    Dear God my lust for death messes with my brain
    Perfection isn't easy but it's something I've achieved
    And I've thrown it all away, so sacrifice me, please
    Crimson blood stains ugly red on my funeral pyre
    And voices screaming in my head, "we love this gorgeous fire"
    Add some pills for fuel as I watch the flames grow higher
    A romantic sort of death upon my funeral pyre

Daughter of Eve

It's red
    The color of my sins
    Displayed bold against my breast
    It defines me as "adulturess"
    I fought, I screamed
    But my pastor won't believe
    That I am innocent
    Because I am
    A daughter of Eve

She Received a Rose

My beauty is but fleeting,
    Like his love sick flowers
    From the moment that they touched his hand,
    They struck a countdown timer
    His gifts are all like poison,
    Corroding through my skin.
    And lovely rose reminds me of the temporary body that I'm in
    I blush and turn away from all affection given,
    My innocence, a virtue,
    Admired by men of heaven
    When I finally fade away, will his love surpass,
    The ugly throes of beauty, that he knew could never last?

Bare Meadow

Planted by the stream
 The meadow idly grown
 Life was a paradise,
 A simple life, a safe home
 One day he came along
 Admired all the flowers
 Stole a thousand daisies
 For a love he scorned for hours
 Left the meadow bare,
 Criticized the weeds
 Went home to his wife
 For forgiveness he would plead
 The simple minded beauty
 Loved her gift of flowers,
 Praised the act of giving
 And placed them in a vase
 They only take up space,
 To remind her of her husband,
 How her love had gone to waste

[My Second Self Was Hurting]

My second self was hurting,
    I could feel his fevered cries
    From the bottom of the ocean
    Where weeks ago he'd died
    From his birth, he was a sailor
    Anchored to his ship
    And when the boat went under,
    His footing never slipped
    He stood command all night
    As the mighty beast went down
    Never touched the lifeboats,
    Lest his legacy be drowned

An Era of Romantics

I am fully convinced
    That if our bodies were to melt away
    At this very moment,
    Our souls would stand together on this earth still.
    You are my act of worship.
    I am devoted to nothing but your soul.

[My Garden Isn't Growing]

My garden isn't growing
    In the way I think it should.
    The roots are all corrupting
    The plants that grow above.
    Weeds spring up so quickly,
    I can hardly match their pace.
    For years I'll fight the battle
    Until I begin to decay,
    Then like long gone seedlings,
    I'll rot and die away.
    From my body will grow flowers,
    In their beauty I will stay.

Fall for a Man Made God

Upon the peak of a distant mountain
    Is where my man did stand,
    An exception to the elements,
    They couldn't raise a hand.
    His brow was sculpted
    By the hands of a godly scholar,
    Placing him up on his own
    Deity-like tower,
    In solitude, he rose his own
    Kingdom devoid of love,
    And suddenly the man did cry,
    For he was not a god.
    The sudden loss of power,
    Broke his spirit bad,
    He begged someone to save him,
    But it echoed off the land
    The moon dipped down
    And grasped his breath,
    Down his solitary mountain, he fell,
    The devilish fingers
    Of the jagged rocks, dragging him
    To the depths of hell
    He was no longer alone- to his own dismay
    He'd always seemed to suffer,
    Always in new ways

The Woman's Fall into Sin

How is it God's perfect creation when my body is a sin?

When his hands found me, it was the moment I caved in?

My skin makes me a temptress, an open invitation

"Come here, come touch me" my body must plead

Because when his big hands found me my mouth froze in a silent scream

And when I begged, "get off of me!" he didn't understand

My life could be so easy without the flaw of man

"But God created humans," my pastor likes to say,

"Divine in his own image, perfect in every way.

But Eve made her husband eat fruit, she caused him to sin"

Adam should have known better, but I do not say a word

I just sit and listen to the preacher's accusations

Because even though he grabbed me, I dragged him through temptations

The shortcomings of man are shouldered on my back

I'll take the blame- I'll take the pain! As long as Jesus stands

"I always will protect you" Is what the Lord would say, but that didn't help me when I wanted to die that day

[Body Washed Upon the Shore]

Body washed upon the shore,
    Disregarded by the sea.
    Greedy hands of water,
    Had lost appeal for me.
    And when I said I hated
    The way it took me in,
    Returned me onto land,
    Where the sand would grate my skin.
    Rocky jagged mountain,
    Watched over where I lay,
    Protecting me from sun,
    Providing only shade.
    Too treacherous to climb,
    I felt betrayed,
    The mighty ocean did return me,
    Yet it was to my dismay.

[Grotesque Contours of Her Face]

Grotesque contours of her face,
Cause me to cringe.
Flinch away from worldly flesh.
Her skin, delicate beneath my hands.
Too soft— she is real. Within my grasp.
And her breathe, the way it sends,
Chills across my body.
Her lips pressed against my thumb.
Dangerous, betrayal of her desire for a kiss.
My interest piques, perhaps she is lovely?
But within her heart, I know-
Burdened by experience, her heart has rotted.
Too many men have touched it,
Mold has begun to grow.
Within her eyes, I can see the ghastly shades of green.
With fingers, slightly hardened from years of work,
She begins to run up my arm.
And although I should avoid it, I let her pull me in.
Too tempted now, I'll become her next sin.
I'm probably the only man willing to take her now,
Perhaps she truly would desire me, even if she were still youthfully lovely and untouched.
But since I view myself through a lens of disgust,
I cannot believe she loves me

[I Trained Myself to Pose]

I trained myself to pose.

    To model my insecurities as promises.

    Advertise myself as an object,

    Untouched by hands of men—

    That added to my appeal.

    I was more desirable when I was seen but not felt.

    When my presence was a mere ghost, my physical being admired by hungry eyes as if I were never even there.

    I feel like a stone statue, sometimes still being carved.

    Mounded and shaped like clay, I watch my body change.

    Opinions of those around me occasionally cutting away my fine slabs of marble.

    Then noticing the lack of womanly curves,

    It is as if my artist builds me back up together—

    New weight around the hips. As he desires.

    I've learned to pose, to emulate art.

    I like to think my semblance to a statue makes me beautiful.

A Best Friends Former Lover

He whispered, like an angel
    In the stillness of the night.
    Trust had been unbroken,
    So it was an unearned right.
    And when he said he loved me,
    In that perfect sort of way,
    I murmured back his promise,
    Despite his unsure gaze
    I wanted him, with passion,
    A religious type of way.
    I don't deserve his love,
    But he doesn't owe me pain.
    And when I said I loved you,
    I felt forced by my own grief,
    It wasn't my feelings for you,
    But the desperation of my dream.

A Kiss You Gave Before I Asked

Lips pressed against my wrist,
    Veins growing warm beneath,
    As if my arm could blush.
    Pale pink, my cheeks glow,
    And my eyes flutter shut.
    Undeserving of your touch,
    I shy, try to turn away.
    But you are solid,
    Man— divinely,
    Strong within your faith.
    So like a soldier, been commanded.
    Take up my burdens as your own.
    Love my body, for it was crafted—
    And the heart within it,
    Made for you alone.

Another Woman's Name

You called me by another woman's name,
  Because she tastes sweeter on your tongue.
  A simple mistake to make, for a man who is in love.
  Too confident of his feelings, they spill out onto others.
  I was originally a bystander, made an unwilling lover.

Baby Crafted From Hate

Madwoman she is,
    Raving about a dead child.
    Didn't we all start this way?
    Hopelessly devoted to a man,
    Who failed to love us.
    We had his children, a compromise.
    He failed to love them too.
    Children die of broken hearts much quicker.
    My baby wasted away, so did yours, as did hers.
    We all start off this way.
    Mad, wild, dejected.
    Subject of rumors, we are reality.
    So weep openly, for love does not look kindly.
    He was not good, nor your child pure.
    Bred from hatred, not passion.
    We all must accept it was never a solution.
    When a man does not want you,
    He puts you in an asylum.
    His problem solved,
    You now need a solution.
    Nothing can heal this shattered marriage.

Divine Masculine

Your face, pressed against the pillow.

The fabric a pale green, your golden curls spilling down.

I tucked your hair behind your ear, as if you were a woman.

Treated you like a lady love.

Perhaps that's why you never took control as a man should.

Your kiss, I know, was sweeter than mine.

The softness of your lips, mixed with the subtle flavor of fruit.

Your hands strayed not to my breasts, but to my thighs,

Claiming that it was where my strength lied.

In a bed, belonging to neither of us,

We played house. The anxious overbearing mother, aloof and absent father.

I saw our future, and chose to still be in love.

The next morning when I woke, I covered fresh bruises with my hair.

I went back to my home, I was only eighteen.

Not a woman, not a mistress, not a wife.

But for one night, I played pretend with you in a bed in someone else's home.

He Doesn't Love Me

I fall slack against you,
    My support— my love.
    And my posture stiffens slightly,
    As you repeat our wedding vows.
    Flowers all around me,
    A garden of our own,
    Reflecting on a venue,
    Where I gave away my soul.
    My hand is clasped in yours,
    You bring it to your lips.
    And give away to me,
    What I read as a timid kiss.
    My palm will hold your feelings,
    But my heart remains untouched.
    I thought "I love you a promise,"
    But only if I am enough.

I Made Him Perfect

He requotes my words in his writing
    But it means nothing, my sweet musings
    Directed towards another woman.
    My romantic longings, plagiarized,
    As I had always dreamed of them to be.
    But in my head, the words I wrote for him,
    Would come back to me, a sense of karma.
    All would be right if he would part his lips,
    And sigh out his unadulterated love for me.
    But instead he thanks me for the inspiration,
    My writings showing him how much he loves her.
    My words can move, change lives,
    Crumble down— ruin me.
    I'm still too scared to tell him I love him.
    That he is always my protagonist,
    And even in hardship I worship him.
    But he takes my words, and introduces her to his beauty instead,
    Despite the fact that I found it myself, buried beneath his foolish
facade.

Religious Fervor

The thorns on his brow pierce my lips
As I give him a tender, comforting kiss
Sweat and dirt mingle on his flesh,
As I take in the pain of his punishment
To suffer so he is not alone,
That is the only fate I know.
My heart shatters as I watch him bleed,
Before his body I fall, on bended knee
To bruise my legs upon the rocks,
To feel some pain his body cannot.
His flesh is marred by earthly scars,
I believed him much above deformities
Illusion shattered as he dies,
The man I love, before me lies.
Put his body in a tomb,
Seal my fate, crucify me too.

Wishing Well

Together we had found a fountain.
    With wishing coins around it strewed.
    And man of fortune, you were seeking,
    What this fount could do for you.
    In greedy fashion you had fed it's,
    Hungry mouth with coins of gold.
    But when it merely drank your riches,
    An uncontrollable anger burned.
    In a rage of passion, you had struck me.
    My skin blistered beneath the heat of your rage.
    Turning your back to my wounded body,
    You went into the woods, away.
    Left alone, my body aching,
    I began to wish for love. And fountain
    Made for those pure wishes, heard my cry,
    And before me came a pretty dove.
    She cried along with me, companionship,
    As I brushed cool water against my skin.
    And as I healed, I saw a man coming.
    Tall and handsome as a prince.
    He took my hand and kissed it gently,
    And took me with him into the woods.
    Together in a dense, dark forest,
    We built a home, a foundation of love.

You Will Last Forever

In a past life I was an artist,
And you were my muse.
Capturing your beauty,
I set it for all to see.
I framed your face, brought your glory.
As the earth was created,
And master wrought up the see,
He placed us in the sky.
You became the sun, and I the moon.
I'm a mere reflection of your radiance.
To make up for a lifetime of my fame,
You have an eternity to claim the world,
Your brilliance radiating from dawn to dusk,
And as you set behind the clouds, there I am,
A reminder that you will come again.
My power has always been to make you more lovely than me.

We Are Both Pawns

You held her in your arms last night.

Held her so close as if she were small, and weak, and just as wounded as I.

Like a child's prized possession, you clasped her to your breast.

As close to your heart as physical possibility would allow.

Distance makes you yearn— close the gap and all is well.

Her smile falters when she realizes the force of your genuine emotion.

Manipulation has made you weak.

She's much smarter than you, conniving.

Playing the role of a life-long lover,

Just so she can watch me suffer.

The Man Who Is My Leader

The forest is enticing,
    The dark depths yet unseen.
    And yet to be the first of men,
    To explore the dangers of these?
    And I one step ahead of you,
    As we forage through the trees.
    It was fear that held you frozen,
    As the branches grasped my hair.
    And fear that held you rooted,
    As I gasped— you were not there.
    And my voice seemed but a whisper,
    In the stillness of the night,
    As stars, they heard my pitiful
    Cry for morning light.
    At the entrance to the jungle,
    You stood waiting for the day.
    At dawn, you'll find my body,
    And in terror, you will cower away.

Mutism

Suddenly, I could no longer write.
    Previously my only inspiration
    Had been that of the idea of love
    Now I have felt it, in true form.
    It is better left off the page.
    Your hands, tangled in my hair.
    My lips, whispering secrets against yours.
    That is love, and it cannot be captured in words.
    Only know that if you died,
    Grief would pierce my heart,
    Sharper than a knife. And I would be gone too.
    This world holds but one good thing.
    Honey, I am obsessed with your soul.
    The gift of loving you is so great,
    It made me forget how to write.
    I hope I never need my words again.

Humor

My voice is drowned out by a theatrical laugh.

My words not important when her humor is invoked.

And despite my attempt at a conversation,

He tells her another joke.

I watch helpless as I lose my standing, receding into the background.

But her giggle is enticing, sounding as if it came from a sunstroke.

So natural, so elegant. I want to be her laugh.

A new desire in me has awoke,

To avoid another heartbreak, I accept my life in the shadows

Relapse

He misses making love to my skeleton
    So I'll lose the weight again
    My body aches for his pleasure
    All the hunger, my endeavor
    Always under constant pressure
    But my life I will surrender

Disease of the Heart

My body rejects him.
	His presence makes me ill.
	Send me out to the sea,
	Away from him, good doctor,
	Please.
	Send me away for a month.
	Watch how I recover.
	Physician, it is him that destroys me.
	I am not dying of disease,
	Other than the rotting of my heart.
	Living things can't rot?
	Doctor, it is dead, broken.
	Save me- prescribe salt air,
	Humid, crashing waves,
	The polluted water that can save.
	Doctor. Please.
	My body rejects my lover,
	It is killing me.

Bouquet

Adorned in proof of your love,
 Yet my confidence is not secure,
 If you cover me in flowers,
 What are you paying penance for?
 Beautiful apology smells like
 Premature decay, these flowers
 Dying in my hands, as my body begins to shake.
 Look me in my eyes, my love,
 Tell me not to fear. Do not look to the ground,
 Where my heart awaits an answer.
 You stare, but not at me,
 Vision fogged as you inhaled.
 Your token of your love for me, is about to fail.
 So flowers dead across my skin, braided in my hair,
 Your voice is broken as you say, "I've let you down,
 I've failed."
 I cry, like any woman would.
 Your sin so great you can't confess,
 All I know is that flowers are a sign,
 Of your unfaithfulness.

He Kissed Me Under The Stars But He Loves Her

When I close my eyes all I can picture is your face pressed tight against hers—

A picture of innocent passion

And although I love you, I will entreat my heart to find a way to forget.

I don't want to corrupt what you have come to define as sacred.

And the unity between two souls,

Is a target that would be best left if it remains unmaimed by me.

So vow yourself to me in the moonlight,

While in the light of day, you belong to her alone.

How I Interpret Love

Assurance sounds solid in my voice.
    I wish that it had come out choked and flat.
    My stupid confidence weighs me down,
    Your eyes flying to my lips,
    Soon followed by yours in a kiss,
    That almost matches the passion of my words.
    Between breaths I want to ask,
    If this means you reciprocate how I feel.
    But then you find me again,
    Pulling me closer to you.
    Our bodies slowly melting into one.
    This must be love.
    Even if you don't say it back,
    You love me enough to become me.
    You sigh against my neck, sufficed,
    Becoming your own self again.
    So physically close. Your heart retreats.
    My head falls to your chest.
    Inside feels hollow,
    Despite the beating in my ears.

Illiterate Men

He tells me that I talk like a book.
    I speak in riddles, and although he means to demean me—
    too confusing, too pretentious— I feel flattered.
    I speak like written words because I am more intelligent than him.
    More romantic, more imaginative, I am more.

Looking Back on Old Pictures

My lips were cracked and dry,
    Dehydrated because my body
    Tried to claim calories from water.
    Stole nutrients from every part of being.
    Looking back, my legs were so small,
    It was a miracle that the protruding bone
    Didn't snap through the bruised flesh.
    And my hair, dyed dark to hide graying blonde,
    Fell out in cascades, the second I tried to brush it.
    When I look back at pictures from two years ago,
    I get jealous of purple bags under my eyes,
    The lack of color in my skin.
    The way I felt empty and proud.
    Now I have hips. Now I have breasts.
    Things I had never before coveted.
    What did I do to deserve this fate of being healed?
    What if I relapse?

Sybil Vane

I understood the musings of nature's grand designs,
    An earthly wizened woman spared from age and time.
    He loved me for my talents and gifted me with praise
    But when my knowledge faltered, he turned from me his gaze.
    A character I've played, life devoted to the stage
    Made emotion out of shadow– enlivened dismal days.
    He brought me to the world, a curtain drawn away,
    I've never been myself, yet my stability he craved.
    Naive as I'd become, I took on a life-long role,
    Unsatisfied, he despised me, I'd lost once perfect form
    So I drank his ugly poisons, died due to his scorn.
    A lovely man has killed me, after showing me the world,
    He embraces wisdom– after I had been his fool.

An Overpaid Translator

Upon request, you inspired me.
Your lips drew pictures, echoing back my stories.
I sat reverent, listening as if absorbing your language.
It was you, translating my words from a foreign tongue.
Like a scholar you understood— inferred love from syllables.
And because you knew, you abused.
You recited my adoration back to me, not from your heart,
But derived from my lips.
Your feigned passion fused into an ugly kiss.

An Ode to a Religious Ex

They accuse me of worshiping a pagan god
    My body melding in his hands as if my flesh is gold,
    Existence becomes a living idol to him.
    Branded across my skin is the sign of his love,
    As he claims more followers through my devotion.
    I am jealous of the others, who get to follow him.
    Does he love them just as dearly?
    Can they please him and pray to him as I do?
    Has anyone ever pleaded with our god in the ways I have?
    Is my love not sacred? Will I never be enough?
    To claim a country, a nation, the world.
    He has big goals for a god who is not real.
    I'll burn my body at his feet, seared red from love.
    In the end, my master, I'll meet.
    I pray there is a good God above.

A Very Pious Wedding Night

Veiled, my face hides a maiden blush.
    This here, my wedding night.
    And candlelight does much to suit,
    The reserved form of a bride.
    My silhouette dances with shadows,
    My husband's solid hands,
    His body has become my rock,
    Our love, a firm foundation.
    My hair it falls in silky streams,
    Around my shoulders, thin.
    My body easily displays,
    My age and innocence.
    To kiss, before, would be a scandal,
    Now it is my goal.
    To taste the lips of my dear husband,
    To feel his touch that I'll call home.

[With the Tidings of a Forced Smile]

With the tidings of a forced smile,
    She timidly takes his hand.
    With proper kiss and bold greeting,
    He proudly meets his bride.
    Her pale white skin,
    Illuminated by glow of innocence,
    Turns to blue beneath his finger tips,
    Deep purple blooms the color of rot.
    As she decays within his grasp,
    Her corpse is labeled 'wife'.
    Each morning he awakes,
    To kiss her back to life.

[Kissing You is like Falling into a Field of Flowers]

Kissing you is like falling into a field of flowers
The virile stems and colorful petals cushioning our descent into hell.
And as I open my eyes, I am greeted not by daisies,
But by the jagged thorns of roses.
My back arched against the pressure of the rocky soil beneath me.
I protest as you pin me down, bodyweight enough to hold me unwillingly in place.
Horror fills me as a serpent crawls among the jagged stems.
With legs like arms, he grabs me, he becomes one with you.
Kissing you is like watching my fate unfold.
My temptation, I pray away, while the devil watches.

To Her Own Demise

Already been discarded,
   By the only man
   Who could ever hold her heart,
   In the palm of once dear hands
   Rough but tender fingers,
   The contrast had impressed,
   Little wide-eyed virgin,
   Now it caused distress.
   The guise had been so plainly,
   Veiled before her eyes.
   She had always seen it coming
   As much as she'd deny.
   So when his death-like grip
   Upon her porcelain heart
   Began to constrict, the longings
   Of her once romantic parts
   She was blind to all these trifles,
   She was a woman after all.
   And he was man almighty,
   To her, he was a god.

[My Body is the Temple]

My body is the temple,
    For our self-sustaining love
    Worship, pure, like heartache,
    I never was enough.
    My fingers, awkward, crooked
    Bony remnants of your crown,
    We worshiped once together,
    Now I'm face down on the ground.
    I beg for your redemption,
    A halfway sacred plea.
    I need your love to wash me,
    Forgive my sins to make me clean

[He Wishes I Were Pretty]

He wishes I were pretty
    Like the girls he tends to love,
    With their silhouetted figures,
    My body seems but rough
    He says that I'm alright,
    He cannot find a flaw.
    I hate the man that flatters me,
    To satisfy his core.
    I know deep down he hates me.
    Finds me rather plain,
    Broken nose on a pale face,
    I wish that I were vain.

Lovers Lament

I felt her love was failing
    I had to make a move-
    Now the scars that mark her arms
    Mar the wooden tomb
    Her body, once majestic
    Now in death is weak
    But she's better off dead
    Than not loving me
    It was only yesterday
    That I realized we were done
    And then in ecstasy,
    I was reaching for my gun
    The bullets never hit
    But twice above her breast
    Now I'm cursed forever
    To feel a lover's lament

Marriage in Hell

We danced the dance of lovers,
    As the poets like to say.
    The intermingling of hearts,
    Two-stepping with a sway.
    I told the man who kissed me,
    That I liked long nights of cold,
    So he held me tight within his arms,
    And carried me down a road,
    A little cobbled path,
    The streets paved in shades of gold,
    Then suddenly we stopped,
    And I watched as hell arose.
    The devil was my husband,
    The man whom I had wed,
    And he brought me to his kingdom,
    To share a marriage bed

Rochester

He was such an ugly man
    With an even grosser heart
    His countenance was vile
    He treated me like dirt
    But something deep within me
    Saw him as a wounded dove,
    A deep desire forming
    To try to win his love
    There was something in the way
    That he held disregard,
    For every other being
    Because of some old 'scars'
    He had a wife he hated,
    So he locked her up away,
    Blamed it on some madness
    Said they were estranged
    I loved him nonetheless
    For something of his flaws
    Drew from me, humanity,
    A simple source of love
    I cared for my contorted man
    With a sense above myself
    And if one ever asked me,
    Our story I would never tell

The Way That Hands Move

The way that hands move when we kiss-
    Nothing left to ground me to the moment,
    But your unrelenting touch,
    Each caress from roughened fingers,
    Is never quite enough.
    Pull me closer to your chest,
    I need to feel your beating heart.
    We're proof that humanity is desperate,
    To draw closer than a touch.

[A Single Flower Left]

A single flower left,
    Untouched by hands of time
    In unadulterated glory,
    Bask in morning shine
    And since it's lovely, share it–
    Admirers divine
    But grasp the thorns not firmly,
    Or my blood will be on thine.
    And accuse me not of malice,
    For you were duly warned,
    My flower, once regarded sacred,
    Is vile for its thorns

A December Date

One flesh, we melt together
    Under an unseasonable sky.
    The burning heat of December,
    Creating one being.
    Breathing together, sinking into the earth.
    Our natural forms- from dust and once again.
    The goal of life attained. To find a soul
    Resembling our own. Then love,
    Together to die.
    Under a sun of reckoning.
    Above the fires of hell,
    Below the jewels of heaven.
    Slowly becoming one on earth.
    Trapped in a purgatory of pleasure,
    Awaiting an eternity where we will be inseparable

A Pastor's Son

The cracks of the mountain,
    Boulders separating, easily placed
    Onto your broad shoulders.
    The gentle crease in your shirt,
    As you bend to lift more.
    To have more of the world pushing on you,
    And as you carry rocks across the mountainside,
    I also whisper my sins into your ear.
    With the weight of my words,
    You fall. Too heavy to bear.
    The whole earth could be comfortably braced in your grasp,
    But the truth my tongue dictates pushes you down.
    Too much, too scared. All that vileness piled into one body?
    Yes. I say, I admit that I feel evil.
    I could never love you, look at me, holy. Like a god.

The Hunger Artist

I once read about a man,
    Who refused to eat
    Locked himself within a cage,
    A show for vulgar eyes
    Then he began to waste away,
    To their dismayed surprise
    Who would have guessed a body,
    Would begin to lose some weight,
    When the possessor is a maniac,
    Fueled by a whorish hungering gaze

Prove My Love

In death your frozen fingers,
Leap across my face.
Adoring the sensation,
Of a life fading away.
I longed to exist among the living,
In a waking, healthy world,
But your corpse is my companion,
It has been since you fell.
Deep within your coffin,
You're pressed against my breast
My hands, slick, with fresh dirt
Are sticky with my sweat.
Your body though unfeeling,
Is desperate for my touch,
Uprooted from your soundless slumber,
So I could prove my love.

My god Died

He was never quite a mortal
That I always knew,
He was very picturesque,
In stature and in form
And the crown across his brow
Did well to adorn,
The very haggard man
Whom all the world adored
As if he were a god.
A god of flesh and bones
Never broken, never bleeding
An all confounding hope
In a man- the thought alone redeeming
Inside his spirit broke,
He'd never let his admirers know
Until one day they found their mortal god,
Dead upon his once holy ground

Bess' Highwayman

My highwayman had promised
    To return by morning light,
    He swore to me most solemnly,
    He'd hid by mask of night
    Then the hooves came riding,
    But it wasn't him at all.
    It was the red troop army,
    And it was his name that they called
    They tied me up against my casement,
    The ropes stung my aching arms,
    But nothing could compare to
    My shattered, broken heart.
    The highwayman had left me,
    Left me good as dead.
    King Georges's army had me,
    Tied up against my bed.
    They taunted and they teased me,
    With their loaded guns,
    Saying that I was the one
    Who would lead the fugitive on.
    But finally, I heard it,
    The cursed and blessed sound
    Hooves against the pavement,
    My love was back in town!
    The army cracked the windows,
    They had their muskets drawn,
    And then in a broken moment,
    I pulled the trigger for a gun,
    I felt it for but a moment,
    Before the world went dim,

I can only hope my lover lives,
Because I died for him.

[It Took a Look of Horror]

It took a look of horror,
    To confess to me your love.
    My death cold hand encased,
    Within your gentle touch.
    And though desperation has grasped me,
    You wouldn't let me go,
    With painted hands, with murder,
    You said I shouldn't be alone.
    So down, past his dead body,
    Decaying in my floor,
    You proposed to me, an offering,
    Your fidelity you swore.
    And I never found my father,
    The tragic, missing man,
    But sometimes through our casement,
    I can hear his body stand.
    And walk about my attic,
    Bones creaking as they move,
    Our wedding night his funeral,
    And our home, his haunted tomb.

[For Every Moment Wasted]

For every moment wasted
    It's a shock there's something left
    The skin clings to my body
    Like it's afraid I'm disintegrating
    Before my untimely death.
    It was the plan all along,
    To slowly fade away,
    But it's dragged on,
    My deaths too slow
    And now I want to see the day

[Cut me Fast and Deep and Hard]

Cut me fast and deep and hard
   Leave me short of breath
   I'll scream your name
   O sweet refrain!
   I'm very close to death
   The blade you used was dull and mean
   With the blunt edge at my throat
   I screamed, I cried, I choked
   Held close inside your gentle arms
   I'll ask "is this revenge?"
   My life come to an end, because you ceased to love me

Bearer

You told me that you wanted me to be the woman who would bear your children.

Knowing that my desire to have a family would be your ticket to physical intimacy.

I thought that because you wanted to create together,

That meant that you loved every portion of me.

Saw all of me as perfect–

You wanted to replicate with me.

You did not love my heart, nor my spirit.

You lusted after my curves, but that is not real appeal.

That is surface-level fancy–

You saw me as the means of satisfaction.

As your soft hands caressed me, I questioned if it was right–

The unholy actions between us.

I prayed that someday they would lead to a good Christian marriage.

Sovereignty on top of sin– I saw no flaw to that plan.

About the Author

Clarice Rider is a pseudonym. The author chooses not to reveal herself so that her work will not be compared against a person, rather a large audience can relate to her work with no background information.